You Lost Me @ Hello

Actionable principles in
relationship marketing

By Donna Smith Bellinger

This book is dedicated to my motivators, the reasons I had to be the relationship builder and breadwinner: my children Clifton and Kristina.

And a special acknowledgement to all those who said it could not be done.

Donna Smith Bellinger

Contact@GroupEndeavors.com

www.GroupEndeavors.com

Cover Art by JMH Creative Solutions

You Lost Me @ Hello

Contents

Foreword

By Dr. David Claerbaut

I have known Donna Smith Bellinger for more than a decade, and now you will have a chance to get to know this wonderful, high-energy, professional woman also.

Her book, You Lost Me @ Hello, is not just another book about sales, talking about prospecting, the right lines to use, presentations, and closing. Yes, there is some very good content on those matters here, but this is really a fresh approach. Donna is on to the single most important element of sales: The first impression.

How many times has someone lost you at hello? A name, a smile, a handshake, a business card, and zero impact. It all fades to black. If you ever have the pleasure of meeting Donna, she will not lose you at hello. You will not forget her. That is no accident. Donna is an expert at making a cordial yet professional impact the instant the clock starts ticking. And she does so with integrity.

Now, she has taken the time to show you—step-by-step—how she does it and how you can do it too. Every single time.

Donna knows the game from the inside. She has been there and back. She is a veteran who has walked the walk in sales and is thoroughly familiar with the journey.

I like a lot of things about You Lost Me @ Hello, more than just the unforgettable title. Donna lets you in on her life—the valleys as well as the mountains—in such a way that she truly becomes your companion in the often lonely world of sales. She also does not waste your time. She gets to the punchline of every important issue—right now. She tells the truth. As you read her book you will see pictures in your mind of exactly what she is saying, because she is so there, so in the real world with her content and examples. And she is fun. This is one of those terrific books that is loaded with substance, yet really fun to read.

So get ready for a good time as well as an informative one. Donna wastes no words. It may not take you long to read You Lost Me

@ Hello; but just like Donna herself, you won't forget her book.

Dr. Claerbaut is an international business consultant and the author of 10 popular and business books.

About the Author

Advancement Strategist Donna Smith Bellinger has successfully inspired, coached, mentored and trained hundreds of people to raise their visibility, laser focus their goals and create a more productive lifestyle. As a mentor, speaker and radio personality, Donna is memorable for her interactive style, upbeat delivery, and ability to connect with audiences on a deep level. Also known for her razor sharp insights, Donna is a master at communicating proven strategies that have helped clients and audiences to create entrepreneurial business models packed with profits and infuse their lives with more fun and freedom.

Her company, Group Endeavors, started as most ideas do, with a conversation, the outcome of which was the statement: "Success is a group endeavor." Building upon that concept, Donna began to actively encourage her audiences to embrace the vision that they should share their strengths with others to further the development of individuals as well as businesses.

Donna's personal mission is to affect more than just the bottom line.

Because Success is a Group Endeavor.

Why This Book at This Time?

This book is for solo business owners and professionals who are struggling to grow their business identity while watching others who may be less talented pass them up on the ladder to more success and more profit. One of the greatest obstacles for emerging businesses is that not enough of the right people know, like and trust them. A major contributing factor to that barrier is that the art of face-to-face engagement (conversation) is dying. And when we do talk, we are boring.

There—I said it.

It's not that you necessarily have a bad product, don't know your stuff, or run poor marketing campaigns. People spend money with people who respect what they value, and they introduce people into their circle of influence that make them look good. Regardless of what is said in the media, new millionaires, great companies and innovative ideas flourish in this economy every day; and you could become one of those success stories, if only the right people knew you existed and were willing to help you to share your story.

Think you are the only one who gets the sweats when entering a room full of people? Millions of people rank networking as one of their greatest fears. There are tons of books that offer insights, factoids, research and the like on the topic, and while they offer valuable information, this can be a very labor intensive way to learn the basic skills that are the foundation of effective relationship building.

My goal for this book is to help you put this fear in its place and develop a mindset that will allow you to walk into any situation with confidence and grace, secure in the knowledge that you will create a memorable impression.

Growing both your career and your business means you must be an open communicator, listening to and sharing ideas and being the person that others want to listen to.

Together we will explore practical tips and strategies to make you more comfortable in both business and social situations as well as help you to uncover the memorable you. These are strategies that have helped me through the years to produce revenue generating results at networking events, memorable impressions in business meetings and forge lasting relationships in life.

It was my ability to create a memorable first impression that helped me to cultivate the relationships that made it possible for me, as a single parent with no college background or corporate experience, to provide for my children. It has opened doors I never dreamed I would enter – let alone be sought after and invited into. And it has allowed me to help other individuals and businesses to grow by showing them how to be the person or company that creates a lasting impression.

Because if you cannot establish a connection, an understanding, a sense of value, then you lost me @ hello.

Not everyone is Going To Like You

Let's get that out of the way. This is not how to win friends and influence people. This is about how to identify the right people for you to connect with, and how to create meaningful and lasting relationships that will be of mutual benefit.

Not everyone will need you. So please don't generalize who you are seeking to connect with. It's not "people with money," "people of influence," or that kiss of death "Everybody!"

A lesson I learned with experience (aka "age") is not only will I not be liked by everyone, but I don't *want* everybody to like me. That's far too time consuming. How many events can you attend, calls and emails can you return, and how many other people's feelings can you worry about? Get a handle on what you truly want to achieve, and create a plan that is inclusive of the values you possess, your talents and your interests.

How? Think Outside the box—

Thinking Outside the Box

In the late 1970's I was already creating a career that was "outside the box." In less than 5 years I had gone from suburban high school student to homeless single-parent. I did factory work, was a corporate administrative assistant, and held a few other jobs before I was blessed with the opportunity that helped me to shape my own style of communication.

An African American single mom in the "new" field of nontraditional or vocational education, I had gone from student to assistant admissions director in less than a year, and with that responsibility came the awesome opportunity to network in a world I had previously not known existed. Now, I had to learn this "business" culture. I was a little more than 21 years old, yet I had responsibilities that required me to communicate effectively with everyone from high school students to old money business owners and everything in between. I was featured in the Chicago Tribune, interviewed on local radio stations and was even the on air voice of my employer's radio ads. This might not mean very much in today's culture, but this was a business world full of blatant racial, cultural and gender biases.

My abilities were not born of any learned skill, but of necessity; I had a family to feed and failure was simply not an option. Besides, ignorance is bliss—I did not know that it "couldn't be done".

So how did a high school graduate with a year and a half of college build an extensive career as a college admissions director, assistant school director, become a top producing sales manager and then go on to start two successful businesses while picking up a few awards along the way? By building a strong network within each industry and having "ambassadors" who consistently challenged me to stretch, reach and grow; wonderful people who had enough confidence in my abilities and integrity that they were willing to put their own reputations on the line to vouch for me without hesitation.

At every event, there are those who seem to draw your attention. I'm not talking about the "stars" of the evening, but those who stimulate conversation by showing genuine interest in what is going on in the room. They seem to project an energy that draws you to them and makes you want to know what they are about. Together, we will explore practical tips and strategies to make you more comfortable and effective in business and social situations as well as help you to uncover the memorable you.

It was my ability to create unforgettable first impressions that helped me to cultivate the relationships that made it possible for me to create and re-create successful careers as well as mentor and guide others.

My motto, "You don't have to struggle, and you don't have to do it alone—success is a Group Endeavor" is a direct result of the path I have travelled.

Once you have clearly identified who you want to be and what you want to attract into your life, you will begin to see that people of similar inclinations will be naturally drawn to you.

What's In It For You?

In order to be successful, you must live your life into your values and your interests; they rely on and feed each other. Why would you want to bother creating a relationship that goes beyond the lifespan of a signed check? What is your desired outcome? Not for an event, but for your life? Too many confuse networking with money and relationships with their personal life. If you are living your life into your values and your interests, then these two are much closer than you think.

You have heard many times that successful people think differently. One of those differences is that successful people know why they do what they do. Successful people understand the value and the consequences of their actions. There is a clear definition of what a desirable outcome is for them in every engagement, decision, and every social or business encounter. They know where the "finish line" is and each success leads to the creation of another wonderful journey.

So what's in it for you? How would your life look if more of your conversations led to relationships? How much richer would your life be if the people you connected with "got" your message, and you were able to be a valuable resource to them in return?

This is the beginning of becoming the person that other people will call "someone you really need to meet."

Why does this seem such a daunting task?

If you have not sold yourself on the benefits of making these connections you allow fear to keep you from reaching your goal. Be sure to identify the benefits you will gain by reaching your goal of connecting with the right people. That is, the people who value you. If you don't commit to your goal 100% you will not maintain the necessary confidence, persistence and enthusiasm to become a memorable you.

Fact: *Having a plan and defined outcomes allows you to clearly define your successes*

Insight: *It's those successes that give you confidence and help you to refine your strategies.*

Relationship Marketing: The Basics

Relationship marketing is an important part of your sales cycle and your career development:

- It's an investment of your time and money
- It's working outside of your comfort zone
- It's market research
- It's selling (yourself and your value)
- It's advertising/branding
- It's customer service
- It's your personal touch

In my seminars and programs we discuss at length the how and why of clearly defining your desired outcomes and working to identify the required actions to achieve that success. I spend a lot of time with my clients to clarify their visions of success, the ideal outcome, and that involves peeling back many layers of goals and visions. For some this is hard to do, because they are always looking for the "magic pill," the short cut, or are just plain resistant to new methodologies. However, knowing what is most important and embracing the ROE (Return on Energy) for taking what might be uncomfortable action are critical steps in creating a successful relationship marketing strategy.

Action Steps:

Note three things that you have gotten from this chapter.

Where have you identified an area that needs improvement?

The Art of Relationship Marketing

Some people like to think that relationship marketing is the same as networking, but they are definitely not the same thing. Networking is a lot like speed dating; elevator pitch, followed by a business card exchange and perhaps a meeting that might lead to a sale.

But to truly grow and sustain your business beyond that one sale, you must develop a relationship with your prospects, clients and the world at large. I have heard business people actually devalue the need of relationships with people they felt would add no value to their business. And I could not disagree more strongly. This is sure fire way to limit your growth as a business and as an individual.

You must get to know people in order to learn what is important to them (their values), what keeps them up at night (their needs), what they plan to do (their goals) as well as who they know.

Would you want to align yourself with a person whose values were in complete opposition to those that you stand for and that you are building your business and personal reputation upon? If you have ever known someone who got "burned" by a client or a business partner, perhaps it was because they were not diligent in getting to know them on more than a superficial level.

Do you track and nurture your relationships; their careers as well as personal interests, support them and their causes, offer advice and seek their feedback? Do you regularly exchange referrals? Through my many years in business, I have formed many wonderful professional relationships. When my partner and I started a technology services firm we grew to over $300,000 in a relatively short period of time based largely on leads and referrals from my relationships, in fact, my database was the reason I was invited into the business.

Relationship marketing is one of the strategies my clients learn to incorporate into their business model to assist them in advancing their careers and creating a business lifestyle that is fun, rewarding and profitable.

Action Steps:

Note three things that you have gotten from this chapter.

Where have you identified an area that needs improvement?

Envision Your Success

No "A" game? Not true, each of us has one. Think to the time you felt most valued. Yes, I said *valued*, not powerful. A memorable first impression is not about power, clothes (sorry fashionistas), or ego; but rather that special essence within yourself that always draws people to you.

Are you ready for your close-up? What will you project when you walk into the room? Will you give off an air of confidence or confusion? When you step into an event, you're making a grand entrance, whether it is a simple coffee meeting or the social event of the year. There is no such thing as slipping in unnoticed, so bring your "A" game each and every time, because you never know who is watching.

A lot has been written about the law of attraction, but that is not quite what I am referring to. Each of us has talents and value that we bring into any situation, however, when we doubt our value we diminish our essence and our power.

In my early days of networking, I had serious doubts every time I walked into a networking event. Usually I was the youngest, least experienced and definitely the darkest in a room of predominately middle-aged white male business men. I didn't know anything about football or golf, I didn't belong to any of their clubs or live in their communities. I felt out of my league, as if I had no purpose, when actually I just did not understand the value of my contributions.

Make the decision to meet one key player at an event, or to meet three new people that fit into your target market. When you achieve that objective, you will find that you are relaxed, open and engaging on an entirely different level during rest of the event.

Envision yourself with those business cards in your pocket, or that key meeting scheduled. Feel the thrill of that success.

Embrace What Makes You Unique

Do you understand how others perceive you? The things that define you are evident in the first moments of conversation. How long does it take to spot ego vs. genuine, real talent vs. wannabe?

Once, at a regional management meeting, I was greeted with this comment: "You must really know what you're doing because they sure did not hire you for your looks!" And nobody stood up for me.

That was an eye opener, and after the shock and terror wore off I realized he was right, I must have been pretty damn good in order to be in that room.

When I learned to embrace my value and appreciate my uniqueness (not my differences or deficiencies), I was able to leverage it to my advantage. This made me a more effective business leader and touched all aspects of my life

With each successful encounter, because I was armed with a clear vision of what would be a successful outcome, my confidence grew. The desired outcome at events was not to win over the entire room, but the key individuals I had identified in my preparation. Soon, I was able walk into any situation fully present to my surroundings, radiating confidence and integrity; a walking magnet for engagement.

Having a plan with defined outcomes allows you to clearly identify your milestones and successes, and it will be those successes that will give you confidence.

By nature I am keenly observant and very inquisitive. I tend to ask pointed questions (even of strangers) and dig into the response. This drives some people nuts (so I don't recommend it for everyone). As a result, I can adapt my persona to the social situation. Are my values still in alignment? Yes, but it's a different side of me (we are all multifaceted). And the engagement is much more strategic.

I suggest you take inventory of yourself before your next event or encounter. Seek input from your colleagues and peers. Here is a wonderful and empowering exercise that will also help to increase confidence and make you a more engaging and fun person. When I have my clients perform this exercise, we do it with two simple questions, and just a quick email does the trick:

Hi _____,

I am working on a personal project and would really appreciate and value your comments on these two questions:

QUESTION 1: Tell me one word that comes to mind when you think of me or describe me.

QUESTION 2: Under what circumstances or in what situation did you see me at my best?

Thanks for your help,

I love visualization exercises. Try these on for size.

- Imagine how it will feel when your business becomes a success.
- Imagine how it will feel to make the correct connections to land that big opportunity.
- Imagine how it will feel when the people you once thought of as unapproachable realize your value and treat you accordingly.

Action Steps:

Note three things that you have gotten from this chapter.

Where have you identified an area that needs improvement?

Be Willing to Leave Your Comfort Zone.

In my ADVANCE U program, one of the principles I stress is that if your dreams do not scare you, if they don't require you to reach deep within yourself to pull out something you never knew was possible, then you are not dreaming big enough. You are still in your comfort zone.

Don't be afraid of making mistakes. Don't quit when things are not perfect. You already own 100% of who you are now, stretch, grow and explore; there's a great big world out there just waiting for you.

Branding Yourself: More Than Just a Pretty Face

What do you stand for?

When you speak, is your conversation worth listening to? Far too often we are presented once in a lifetime (or so we think) opportunities and it becomes a case of open mouth – insert foot. You must be totally comfortable with your values and your desired results. Your aim is not to be the center of attention, but to be interesting to the people that you desire to connect with.

- What is their first impression of you (what do you radiate)?
- What about the encounter was memorable?
- What did you learn from the encounter that was useful?
- Who are your "ambassadors" in this encounter (who is on your side)?
- In what ways will you develop this relationship?

How Are You Perceived?

Consider the image that you project. In my workshops I ask my participants to visualize the dollar value of their dream sale, whether it is a specific position you are targeting within your career or a product / service for your business.

Got that number in your head? Now, go to a mirror, and think "would you give that money to the person looking back at you?" Does the image in the mirror instill confidence, capabilities and integrity? Would your image appeal to the person you need to connect with? How would it compare to the people that they are already doing business with?

Fact: *We do business with people we know, like and trust.*

Insight: *For most of us perception equals reality.*

It's Not the Shoes

In face-to-face communications, words, tone and body language are the determining factors in how you are perceived.

There is an often debated theory called the 7% – 38% – 55% rule. This rule states that 55% of our communication is though body language, 38% in our tone, and only 7% in our words. We have all seen this in play. Even though this rule is not 100% reliable, there are some fundamental truths here.

How often have you been introduced to someone who is so busy posturing for non-existent paparazzi and looking for someone more important than you to speak with that you don't even want to bother to exchange information?

When you dig into your memory to recall a recent conversation, how much of it actually comes to mind? If you are pulling a note out for a business reason, it is probably for one specific statement that stuck with you. Were they humorous and intelligent or self-absorbed and boring? In short, how well did that person's first impression reflect the values you want associated with you? Are they a person you would want to represent you (send referrals to) or that you would stake your reputation on by introducing them to your circle?

Think now of the person who is gracious, attentive and genuinely pleased to meet you. Their discussion is not centered on themselves, rather they are actively engaging all members of the conversation. How do you want to be remembered? In most circumstances, I have found this person to be the better connected, better liked, and more productive relationship to pursue. Why? Well, if I would like to do business with them, other like - minded people might feel the same way.

Action Steps:

Note three things that you have gotten from this chapter.

Where have you identified an area that needs improvement?

Successful Connectors Think Differently

Too often I see self-proclaimed power networkers playing the "speed dating" game with their business cards; how many did I get, or give out? It has been said in many different ways, "you have to give in order to get." People do business with those they know, like and trust. The bottom-line is that if you do not value the person you are facing there will not be a positive connection, and a positive connection is the desired outcome in any conversation, a mutually beneficial exchange of information and ideas – a relationship!

Unless I am at a conference or similar major event I don't carry a lot of business cards on me. This is because I don't generally give them away. If within our conversation, we strike a chord or connection and we are willing to exchange information in order to take the conversation further, I have a business card at the ready. You see, I am not looking for more junk emails. I am looking for people I can develop a relationship with who share values that are compatible with mine or with the people I am already connected to, because I understand what my contacts are looking for.

It's been said that it's not what you know but who you know that determines your success, however that's not quite accurate.

It's what you know *about* who you know, and I don't mean the skeletons in their closet.

I have spent many years in corporate sales, and learned a variety of techniques for setting appointments, conducting meetings, closing the sale, following-up, you name it I've been there and probably taught a course on it.

Start by placing value on the opinions of others (alright, some people might not deserve it – but at least let them put their foot in their mouth and confirm it before you tune them out). The skill of listening attentively and actually appreciating the value and the values of the other person, especially when they differ from yours, is a skill that has been honed by all highly successful individuals.

But one of the most valuable lessons to be learned is often overlooked in business development. What is their "why?" Understanding the "why" is the key differentiator between someone you meet, and someone you engage.

Understanding the "why," whether it is to communicate more effectively with your family, your employees, or anyone else, is the key to creating a two-way dialogue that produces a mutually beneficial relationship. This is why some of the most abrasive people still seem to succeed. Because they understand and leverage the "why."

Become a Gracious Listener

In this digital age, true communication is falling by the wayside in the maze of tweets, texts, and posts. The lively art of conversation is quickly evaporating.

Families are no longer engaging in conversation, they hand the child a cell phone or tablet computer so they can text and tweet in peace. On a recent trip to Disney World, I observed a family of 6, with children ranging from 3 years of age to teenagers, at lunch. Each person at the table was staring at their own electronic device, completely ignoring the other people at the table for the entire duration of the meal.

In relationship marketing the key word is relationship, and in order to develop a successful relationship you must communicate.

Indeed, we can have wonderful conversations around key issues that are important to us. Did you get that? We welcome discussing issues important to *us*, but what about the interests of the *other person*? Do you take the time to find out what they are truly interested in? Why did they choose to attend the event? Were they interested in the topic or was it an obligation? What would they rather be doing and why?

In one workshop, I had among my attendees a couple that had been married for decades and raised wonderful and successful children. At the end we discussed interests that we had never shared or pursued. The wife voiced her dream and her husband literally spun in his chair! He was amazed that after all this time, he never knew how much she cared about that topic.

It's not your wardrobe, car or zip code that attracts supporters, clients, and the person with who has the influence, knowledge – or the check. Without a doubt the most effective tool in your relationship marketing arsenal is the skill of being an effective listener. Never mind the elevator pitches and the "shark tank" explanations of your business and its benefits. When you listen intently to the conversation of your new contact, you will pick up all of the data you need to determine how to best create the basis of a relationship with this individual or if he or she is a person who is in alignment with the people you want to include in your circle of influence. Of course the answer is not always "yes."

Have you ever attended a networking event, done the " speed dating" thing and collected a bunch of business cards and when you go through them the next day, you can't remember who many of them are or what your conversation was about?

At the end of every engagement, you should be able to identify the following:

- What was your first impression of them?
- What made the encounter memorable?
- What did you learn from the encounter that was useful?
- In what ways would you develop this relationship?

These questions can only be answered if you are an attentive listener. Be honest, how many times have you left an event and had no idea how to leverage all the business cards you collected?

Fortunately for me, I was raised in a generation where children were trained to be "seen but not heard." So in my case, I became an observer at an early age; passively absorbing and processing all I could. That made me an expert on family gossip and translated well into my professional life.

And here is a special tip.

Knowing your communication style is a distinct advantage when engaging others. I am a people watcher, and I often find it entertaining to watch others morph through one or two styles during the course of an event, although I see it occur most often pre-and post meetings. As I describe these styles you will surely see yourself in certain situations. For more in depth discussion regarding persuasion styles, I highly recommend *The Art of Woo: Using Strategic Persuasion to Sell Your Ideas* by G. Richard Shell and Mario Moussa. This book contains several self assessments that will give you another level of insight into what you project and also aids you in deciphering the signals of others.

Being able to "read" others is an invaluable skill; you don't need to be a "profiler," but understanding what motivates others will go a long way toward winning them over to your side when you have a specific outcome in mind. If you ever watched children with their parents you may have noticed that they develop great skill in manipulating situations to their advantage, one parent may respond to tears and the other to some other tactic.

Knowing your communication style and knowing how to manage the styles of others can reduce conflicts, increase productivity, and improve teamwork in the workplace. If you are aware of your dominant communication style, it will enable you to discern how it interacts with other types and you will have more control over how others perceive you.

There are numerous tools such as the Myers Briggs Type Indicator[1] that can be used to determine your style. I frequently include this type of work in my programs – it is a deal MAKER!

---

[1] MBTI, Meyers Briggs and MyersBriggs Type Indicators are registered trademarks of the Meyers-Briggs Type indicator Trust in the United States and other countries

Fact: The image you project becomes your personal brand.

Insight: This is not the Red Carpet. Cover the cleavage, remove the Bluetooth, and turn off the cell phone. You rarely see a truly successful person glued to their phone at an event.   A successful person's processes are so tight that they don't have to serve their business, the business serves them.

Action Steps:

Note three things that you have gotten from this chapter.

Where have you identified an area that needs improvement?

"Who Are You Going to Believe, Me or Your Lying Eyes?"

If we have a choice between believing the words we hear or the behavior we observe we go with our eyes every time. Consider the image that you project.

I cannot begin to count the events I have attended where I see images that are directly opposed to the objectives of the evening. Cover the cleavage, remove the Bluetooth and turn off the cell phone. Do you reflect the image of the person you need to connect with? What about the image of the people you have uncovered in your research that they are already doing business with?

It is a painful fact that most of us simply do not see ourselves through the eyes of the people we communicate with on a daily basis. As a whole people are quick to judge, and it's acknowledged that a first impression is formed within the first seven to ten seconds of a greeting.

You may reflect the latest fashions to your peers, but in doing business you must be careful to reflect your values as well as your fashion sense. In our messaging, our lips may say "I am so pleased to meet you," while our body language sends a very different message such as "I'm nervous" or "I wish I wasn't here" or "you are so boring."

When I attend events, I listen with both ears. One is tuned to things that I can make happen in the near future, and the other ear is tuned to opportunities that, while they may not currently fit my needs, are worthy of saving for another situation or another of my contacts. And generally I listen twice as much as I talk. That in itself gets the attention of the other individual and it saves me time because I am not engaging in a conversation that is not meeting my desired outcome for that specific event.

This all takes patience and work. Sometimes it can feel like pulling water out of a rock, and other times it opens the floodgates to ideas, inspiration and profit.

Good News Travels Fast – Bad News Travels Faster

The key to excellent results-driven connecting is giving, not receiving. When someone does something nice for you, it is natural to want to reciprocate. On the other hand, we all know someone whose calls we avoid (aka "duck") because we know they will be a negative to our resources (time and/or money).

Preparation meets opportunity

Part of my objective here is to give you the foundation to walk into a situation with confidence and grace, secure in the knowledge that on some level you will be able to create a memorable impression. What we're going to do now is identify what may be preventing you from moving through these business and social circles with ease and with comfort.

Sometimes it pays to be bold.

I was determined to meet the head of an organization. There was already a business relationship between one of my firms and hers. She was notorious for only meeting "A" list people, however, I was not deterred. I confidently stood at her receiving line – careful to let all of the "top dogs" precede me, one, out of respect and two, I didn't want any witnesses if it blew up in my face.

As we shook hands and I fully introduced myself mentioning the projects that we had in common, she coolly assured me that she had spoken longer with me in that instance than any of the others I'd mentioned and she walked away. However, every time we encountered each other thereafter, I was greeted warmly and with recognition. Why? Because my boldness "wowed" her *and* I kept the encounter to myself. Could I have contributed to gossip? Absolutely, but it would have done nothing to get me closer to my goals, in fact it would have damaged my reputation much more than hers.

You can't make this stuff up.

In another instance I attended a networking event where as an ice breaker everyone in the room had to poll the other attendees and get answers to questions that had been given out by the facilitator. I approached a woman who was standing off to the side with my usual confidence and one of my most winning smiles. Her cool response was "I spoke to someone on the train coming in here, do I still have to talk to people?" I moved on to more fertile ground. That was not a rejection, it was a gift. I saved 5 minutes of connecting time and since I knew my value, she did not burst my confidence bubble at all.

On the upside, I have had thousands of conversations that began with a simple "what brought you here tonight," and resulted in new clients and new opportunities.

When you walk into an event and don't have a real connection with anyone in the room, you have a tendency to sit back and wait for things to kind of come to you, sort of like a guest waiting to be served. However, if you assume a more active role, you'll find that you're going to have a much more rewarding experience. Some ways that you can do this would be to find the organizer and ask if they need any assistance. One of my favorite things to do is to volunteer to greet at the door. Do I miss out on the food? Possibly. But I also learn who's who and where they will be seated. That information can be priceless when it comes to working the room later on.

You also want to look for the most approachable person in the room. And beyond that, you want to look for the person who is attracting or exhibiting their "wow" to the people in the room. You know what I mean. You can walk into a room and just feel that there's something happening over in the corner with that particular person. And your thought is "I really need to find out why everyone wants to talk to that person." So you move over to that area and listen in on that conversation. Perhaps you might pick up a couple of tidbits that would enable you to decide if you would like to meet this person later.

Still shy? Use those tidbits as an ice breaker. You may want to wait until the crowd around them thins down a little bit, circle back and say "excuse me, we haven't met yet, but I overheard you talking about blah, blah, blah, and I wanted to come back and introduce myself to you and tell you how interesting I found that to be. Would you be willing to share a bit more, because I didn't hear the whole thing—?" And that can be the beginning of a wonderful conversation, because listening is "key" when you are beginning to establish a relationship.

Networking is reciprocal. And it doesn't run on a timetable so don't disregard someone that you feel is perhaps not important enough for you to listen to. Because you never know who they may know! They may be the executive assistant to the person who's eventually going to give you the biggest contract you've ever had. They could be the first cousin to your boss, or someone else that you're trying to get close to. Always be charming, and attentive and graceful, even when you have to make an exit or extract yourself from a situation.

How to Prepare for Your NEW Normal in Relationship Marketing

Assessing the value of an event

I get invited to at least 20 events every month. As a self preservation tactic, I created my own system to best leverage my marketing time and dollars, since most worthwhile events have some type of associated cost even if it is just wardrobe and transportation.

By relying on this "priority list," I can simplify my ROE for these events. I rank invitations in 4 categories:

1. Business opportunity: meetings and presentations
2. See and be seen: events to support friends or causes I want to support
3. Strategic appearance: events I attend as a part of doing business
4. Informative: attending speeches, workshops, seminars, trade shows

When considering the value of an event ask yourself:

- WIIFM (What's In It For Me) Why do I need to attend?
- Who are the key players? How can I leverage this event to my advantage?
- Is this time sensitive to a current goal of mine?
- Are the attendees critical to my immediate goals?
- Is it in alignment with my values and interests?

Many other useful tips can be found in my audio book "Creating the 8th Day and the 5th Hour" available at:

www.groupendeavors.com/products

Leave Your FEAR at home

"I can't do it because I don't know any-body"

"I'm not interesting (or not interested)"

"What if they don't like me?"

Sound familiar? It's that small voice try-ing to program you into believing that you are less than your best. Whispering that you have already done your greatest work and there is nothing more to look forward to.

That is just fear. Ignore it. None of these things have anything to do with your ability to create a relationship, and we're going to address each of these concerns in turn. And if it makes you feel any better, *everybody* has that little voice, it is just a matter of whether you manage it, or you surrender and allow it to manage you. But, that's another book.

It's been said that a journey of a million miles begins with the first step. Your goal is not to get to know everyone in the room, just one or two people who meet your interests or your needs. This is why you must have a strategy regarding your objective when you attend an event for business purposes. Having your objective clearly placed in your mind will direct your actions and your attitude throughout the event.

Becoming More Memorable

The most nerve wracking part of any new introduction is the "elevator pitch". Does it scare you to death? It won't if you are prepared. Ever try to think of someone you met and had a conversation with, but you can't remember their name or their business to look them up? Well, you certainly don't want to be one of those "unmemorables" do you?

It's all well and good to pass out business cards, but if people don't remember you, they probably won't be calling to follow up, and they certainly won't keep you in mind for their future needs or possible referrals.

Also, don't use the same opening for every person— huge mistake, it sounds a little like begging. "This is what I do—please like me!"

Strategy is Essential

Over the years, I have learned what to do – and what not to do; I have often joked to my children that I am a walking example of "Don't Let This Happen to You!" Part of my objective here is to help you shorten your learning curve and assist you in getting to "memorable."

Understand your value and communicate it in a manner that allows your message to touch the areas that are of interest to the person you are addressing.

Action Steps:

Note three things that you have gotten from this chapter.

Where have you identified an area that needs improvement?

Can You Hear Me Now?

When you WOW people, they not only remember you, but they keep you in mind for their future needs or perhaps even referrals. How do you know what is of interest to them? Ask probing questions and LISTEN. Too often we spend our time waiting for a chance to speak. Keep your eyes only on the person you are talking to. Do not scan the room for your next "target." When people feel that they are being "heard," it changes their energy and the energy of the situation.

Example:

"Hi, what brought you here this evening?"

"I am very impressed with what this group has achieved and thought that by attending I might learn more about how my background might be of service to the organization."

"Really, what do you do?"

"I assist people in increasing their performance and visibility in individual and team settings."

Not a hard pitch and the doors are open for further discussion, like "How do you do that?" or "Who have you worked with?" And if *you* are on the receiving end of this conversation try something like "Tell me about your most challenging or rewarding experience."

Identify one portion of what you do that will speak to the situation. If you own a salon or offer related personal services (like massages) and are attending a woman's event you might speak to helping overworked business owners in their search for work life balance. Speak of the outcome for the client after they have purchased from you and use that as your lead in. A friend of mine who is amazing at photography and specializes in major events refers to her services as a chronicling of history in visual format. She captures once in a lifetime moments.

"I can't do it because I don't know anybody"

Working a room is nothing to fear. It's actually just the first level of networking, and you do that on the first day of school, or camp, at weddings, on vacation, or wherever, when you start to look everything over and determine who it is you really want to get to know, sometimes with a great deal of success and other time with a more than a little pain.

Here's a tip: Position yourself in a specific location. A dynamo of the women I encountered at one of my first large conferences had a wonderful way of ensuring that she had the opportunity to engage as many people as possible. What was her brilliant tactic? She stationed herself near at the head of the buffet line. From there she personally greeted and chatted up folks as they waited in the inevitable bottleneck. Was she passing out her material? Not at all – she took many cards however and scheduled follow-up chats.

Another tip: Volunteer to be a host or hostess or any of the un-glamorous jobs nobody wants to do. You gain a reputation of being giving, get to meet lots of interesting people, and get invited to a lot of other events. This is especially helpful if it is a budget—breaking event you might not otherwise have attended.

Still shy? Find someone who is doing the same thing you are, eating the same dish, having a similar drink, or perhaps also reviewing the program. You have just found something you have in common, go for it.

At last! You get to meet "your target" person, and they are impressed with your story and want to have a further discussion—
high five! Here's their card and please forward your resume, marketing kit or white papers. Are you ready to fire that off tonight? Not a week from now—not under development—but right now! A part of establishing your creditability is being able to deliver on your promises.

Some Simple Courtesy "Do's" and "Don'ts" at Events

- Don't forget to RSVP (and don't forget to decline or cancel).
- Do always arrive early (The party is always before the party).
- Do dress the part; if you want to be taken seriously, leave the club wear, "bling" and Bluetooth at home.
- Never arrive at an event hungry, who wants to shake a greasy hand? And save the libations as a celebration of achieving your objective. You don't want to meet the most important person in the room slurring your words and spilling food. Toast your success after you WOW them.
- Don't do a hard sell; events are ice-breakers, the meeting is for closing deals. This is an opportunity for you to show your personal side, your worth, and integrity.

Action Steps:

Note three things that you have gotten from this chapter.

Where have you identified an area that needs improvement?

How to Remember Why You Wanted The Card in the First Place

I have a rule: I never give a business card out to a person who does not ask for it. Does that mean that I don't give out my cards? Not at all. And do I collect them? You bet! But this way each card has meaning attached to it.

As a rule you do not write on the card in the presence of the offerer—however, there are exceptions: it may be appropriate to make a note on the card itself, for instance if they are referring you to someone and you need to get the name and phone number during the conversation and you want to be clear of the source.

Men usually separate level of importance by the pocket they place the card in. One for "toss it", another for "follow-up" and usually the inside breast pocket for "the money card."

In our effort to be fashionistas, most women are out with a small bag and precious few cards, so here are my tips:

If this is a general follow-up–a person who was so eager to meet you that they have already requested your card, ask them to send you a LinkedIn invitation and take it from that point.

A warm introduction–introduced to you or referred to you by someone you have a relationship with–I gently dog-ear the corner of the card

A hot follow-up–fold the card in half. Even when you straighten it back out to fit in your card holder (that is where the money cards go) you will recognize that card instantly for what it represents.

Being Prepared to be Successful

You should have several versions of your follow up message prepared to provide upon request. Update your online presence, review your LinkedIn profile, clean up your Facebook page, and review your website.

Establish a system for tracking your progress, whether you chose a full blown CRM such as Salesforce.com; a spreadsheet like Microsoft Excel or a database like Microsoft Access, or any of the many cloud /mobile applications available. Chose one and use it faithfully. The key word here is consistency.

I was hired to assist an established firm through a lunch and learn to improve their follow-up and closing techniques. My request was simple; bring your call sheets or tracking system with you to the meeting. Once everyone (including the owner) was assembled, no one had anything to put on the table; where was the business? I do working trainings and we were going to use exactly the leads they were complaining about. When the request was repeated, staff had to head to cars, look under calendars and pull cards from their purses and wallets.

We stopped at that point and I had a conversation with the owner that resulted in a 6 month contract to re-vamp the sales process. Their business grew not just locally but internationally through relationships and referrals.

Hot Tips:

Immediately— not later—add the contact to your database.

Always review the contact prior to sending a LinkedIn invitation; see who they are connected to. If they have a profile, review it. This will lay the foundation for your next meeting and assist you in creating your "ask."

Have several versions of your marketing materials available so that you can customize your response to the context of the initial conversation.

Follow up within 24-48 hours when possible.

I send a personal note no later than the next morning, if the mailing address is available on their card. If not, email is next option, and within a week, I leave a voice message.

My voice message (or handwritten note) is simple:

Greetings John,
It was a pleasure to meet you at the
_____. I regret that we did not
have more time to chat about your interest in
_____. (This is something THEY said they
were interested in, NOT your business, unless
it was requested).

Is there a convenient time for a follow
up call or coffee meeting?

Best Regards,
Donna Smith Bellinger
PS, Please look for my invitation to
connect on LinkedIn.

Nothing Replaces the Personal Touch

What impresses you more, an automated call or a live person? An email versus a handwritten note? In this high-tech age it can be challenging to differentiate yourself. Injecting the Personal Touch into all of your interactions will earn you a bit of distinction.

Like all things of great value, a certain amount of care and maintenance is required to maintain and grow relationships. The care you take in developing the initial contact becomes even more important as you explore new levels of connection.

This is where your individual personality comes in. Frankly, I am not one of those birthday and anniversary type people. So I am not known for that kind of follow-up. However, a dear friend of mine is the total opposite. Opal is the Queen of Cards, Hallmark Cards, and they must have the little gold seal on the envelope. Thank you cards, miss you cards, and all of the required holidays. She is awesome.

Another extremely successful friend of mine excels in the art of the phone call. He returns every message, but never before 3pm. My circle knows the best time to reach me directly is between 6:30am and 10:00am, after that it's pretty much email and texts. I make business calls between 10:00am – noon on certain days. My schedule is rigid due to the private clients I service and my speaking/media obligations.

What is the culture of your contacts? Learn and respect their patterns and requests. I do at least 2 breakfast meetings a week (7 am) and hardly any lunch dates. However, if that is what your prospect requires, make the occasional adjustment.

Place yourself in their path as often as possible; be aware of the groups, clubs and organizations they support.

Be a researcher. Learn what you can so that you can be of more value both to them and to yourself. Once they open doors to their circles, you have to be equipped to do the only thing that matters to them, make them look good for introducing you!

And the pattern repeats itself.

Special note: In the world of relationship marketing, quality and constancy are Queen. You are your word; make no promises you cannot keep. There is no harm in saying "I'll see what I can do" rather than "sure I can do that!"

Action Steps:

Note three things that you have gotten from this chapter.

Where have you identified an area that needs improvement?

You Don't Have to Walk Alone, Relationship Marketing is a Group Endeavor

Creating Supporters and Ambassadors

The *Encarta World English Dictionary* gives the following definitions for support:

- Keep something or somebody stable: to keep something or somebody upright or in place, or prevent something or somebody from falling
- Enable something to live: to provide sufficient food and water or the appropriate conditions or facilities to enable people or animals to live or allow something to function
- Give active help and encouragement: to give active help, encouragement, or money to somebody or something

Your supporters are those who help you frame and nurture your dreams and goals. You need supporters both professionally and personally. Your supporters spark ideas, share information, open doors and help you to know when a door needs to be closed.

Supporters are not one size fits all. I have supporters or mentors for many different areas of my growth and development. Some of them don't even know that they coach me– it's an awesome burden to knowingly take on that responsibility, and after all, they have their own lives; and besides, how do you feel when you advice is ignored?

Of course everything that is good to you is not good for you. A true supporter is not a "yes man" or groupie. Chose at least some of your supporters from a group that is already in the lifestyle or business style you are reaching for.

It is important to create a network of Ambassadors and trusted advisors, however you don't select them; they choose you. Your Ambassadors are those who help you frame and nurture your dreams and goals; both pro-fessionally and personally. They also spark ideas, share information, open doors and help you to understand when a door needs to be closed.

Often in my writings I talk about your Fab 5—the five people you keep closest who inspire motivate and kick butt in their area of expertise. It has been said that we are the average of the five people we spend the most time with. You can't fire everyone from your life that doesn't meet the Fab criteria, but you must have that circle in your life. My five are in different parts of the world, different races, genders and ages, and I learn from all of them regularly. Not all are in business; some are educators, pastors, and just plain folks. They bring me so much joy!

One of my favorite people, Sandra Yancey, founder of eWomen's Network, once gave me this advice: "Surround yourself with people who accomplish easily the things you struggle to achieve."

As you progress in your career or business, those types of mentors are going to become easier to come by, because they will be seeking you out!

"I don't know the key to success, but the key to failure is trying to please everybody."

~ Bill Cosby

This quote from Bill Cosby is so accurate when it comes to creating long-lasting relationships. You do not have to be everything to everyone, so do not put that burden upon yourself. You are a fascinating multifaceted individual and it is your individuality that will help you to create the relationships that will help you to grow your career, your business, and improve your life.

There will be those you will seek out as mentors; and those who will seek you out to mentor them. Over the course of your career and you will be both the giver and the receiver, so build a reputation that will have others seek you out not only for what you can do for them but for what they can offer to you in return.

There are a few basics that you must master in order to build these priceless relationships.

First: Remember that you are your word. To create memorable relationships, you must be of exceptional integrity. Many people make promises but few deliver. Don't be afraid to say I can't or I won't. Making false promises, being out of integrity, can make you memorable as well. Who wants to recommend the person, or put their own reputation on the line for someone who is not trustworthy, who does not honor their promises, or their commitments? If you say you are going to call back within 24 hours, do it.

Second: be consistent in maintaining the relationship. It's this is not as labor intensive as it sounds, but keeping in regular contact beyond the holiday cards is imperative in maintaining your relationships. Beyond the updates of your latest accomplishment, do you take the time to keep up with the accomplishments of others? Are you aware of their interests and their needs? Do you invite them into your circles and graciously facilitate introduction and connections?

Third: be confident in the quality of your contributions.

Fourth: create the messages that make you memorable. Being able to label your uniqueness makes it much easier for your missionaries to focus on areas that would be of value to you. Have them think of you in terms of the labels identified when you polled your peers. Secure your personality strengths and traits with labels such as: team builder, thought leader, organizer, and innovator.

Last: Be a cheerful giver. Be giving of your time, and your talents.

I have met far too many people who have an attitude of "what's in it for me?" but the truth is you get what you give many times over. Gifts of time that were shared years ago have turned into showers of blessings at the times I needed them the most.

Find your style, find your joy and share your authentic self with the world. Give me the real you, otherwise—

You lost me @ hello

Bonus: Hosting Your Own Events

What an easy way to re-introduce yourself into society.

Never be at a loss for new things to try to create an interest for your clients and potential clients. You want to invite as many people as possible to your events for three important reasons:

- You want to leverage your time so you're connecting with as many quality contacts as possible in the shortest period of time.
- You want to leverage the power of communities. When you bring people together, they create far more energy and excitement than you can on your own. Your guests will also see other people interested in what you have to offer, and that's the best way to build credibility.
- Be a generous connector. If you're known as someone who brings people

together, it will help you build your reputation and increase your likability.

My special gift to you is my three part audio series: "Why Didn't That Work"

Claim it by visiting:

www.groupendeavors.com/free-gift

Your password is: **advanceu**

Would you like more?

I invite you to request a no obligation Discovery Session with me so that we might explore how we might support each other.

Make your request by visiting
www.groupendeavors.com/discovery

Book Donna Smith Bellinger to speak at your next event

Group Endeavors LLC
105 W. Germania
Chicago, Illinois
866-208-3254 phone and fax
Donna.smithbellinger@groupendeavors.com

Include the following information:

Name_____

Address_____

Email Address _____

City, State, Zip _____

Country_____

Phone_____Fax_____

Request:_____

Acknowledgements

To my Hubby Bear, Steve Bellinger, for performing an act of emergency c-section to bring this book into the world.

I must thank "The Girls:" Karyn Pettigrew, Cynthia Williams, and, Hadassah Hickman for backing me in a corner with a real intervention and helping me find my joy.

Much gratitude to Dr. Joel Martin for her unwavering faith and tough love.

Special hugs and thanks to Hazel Palache, my first real coach. I took a part-time job to pay her fee and have never looked back. She placed me at the top of the stairway and changed my life forever.

My sisters from my Heavenly Father; Opal Freeman, Deborah Crable, Pepper Miller and Marquetta Glass.

And hugs to my daughter supporters Jetta Bates, Janice Bond and Julie Holloway. My other "kids" get the next book ☺.

And my brothers Lester McCarroll, James Summers, LeRoy Kennedy, Andrew Morrison, Jeff Meade and Ken Smikle.

Read more from
Donna Smith Bellinger and
other entrepreneurs in
The Entrepreneur Within You
Volume 2
Coming 1.1.14!

JOIN THE TEW MOVEMENT
www.tewyou.com
twitter.com/tewyou
#TEWmovement

EMPOWERING. EQUIPPING.
INSPIRING.

Made in the USA
Lexington, KY
13 September 2013